Who Left The Ladder Of Success in the Middle of My Failure

Drew Wohlford

Introduction
The Imperfect Climb Up the Ladder (With a Few Rungs Missing)

Have you ever felt like you're constantly scrambling up a ladder, only to find out it's been leaning against the wrong wall the entire time? Yeah, that's my specialty. And if you can relate, then congratulations! You're in good company. This book is for anyone who's ever felt like they're barely clinging to the ladder of success, with a few rungs missing and a pesky squirrel nibbling at their shoelaces.

Let me illustrate. Picture this: I'm at the grocery store, attempting to be a responsible adult and buy some kale. But as I'm reaching for that leafy green goodness, my foot slips on a spilled jar of marinara sauce (because of course it was). Down I go, my arms flailing like a flamingo having a seizure. And in that moment, instead of the usual embarrassment, I just burst out laughing. Because honestly, what else can you do when you're sprawled out in the produce section, surrounded by judging vegetables?

That's the spirit of this book. It's about embracing the ridiculousness of our failures, the humor in our hiccups along the way. Because let's face it, the journey up the ladder of success is rarely a straight shot to the top. There are going to be slips, trips, and face-plants in the kale. But it's how we respond that matters.

So if you're ready to laugh at your mistakes, to find the humor in your hiccups, and to keep on climbing (even with a few rungs missing), then buckle up, friend. We're in this together. And who knows, we might just find that the view from this ladder is a lot better than we thought.

Chapter 1

I'm a big believer in the whole "when life gives you lemons, make lemonade" philosophy. It's all about turning those sour moments into something sweet. But what happens when you take that lemonade and spill it all over your shirt? Or your pants. Or your important work presentation. Well, that's more my speed.

You see, I'm not just talking about your run-of-the-mill, everyday failures. I'm talking about the spectacular, laugh-out-loud, face-palm-inducing kind of failures that leave you wondering, "Who left the ladder of success in the middle of my failure?" The kind that make you want to crawl under a rock and hide, but at the same time, you can't help but laugh at the absurdity of it all.

Take the time I tried to make a good impression on my first day at a new job. I woke up early, carefully picked out my clothes, and even managed to get there a whole 20 minutes before I was supposed to start. Feeling pretty good about myself, I stepped up and reached for the door handle...as I hear a rip. Of course, I split my pants, not a small split but all the way up the back and part way up the front. I looked like I was trying to start a new fashion trend.

    Standing there, the wind blowing through my underside , I had a choice to make. I could let my embarrassment get the best of me and call in sick, or I could own that split like it was a badge of honor. So, I took a deep breath, walked into the office, and introduced myself to my new coworkers. "Hi, I'm Drew, the new inside sales guy. I see I've already made a big impression."

It wasn't how I envisioned my first day going, but by laughing at myself and the absurdity of the situation, I was able to turn what could have been a disaster into a funny story that broke the ice and helped me connect with my new team.

We all have those moments, the ones that make us want to crawl under a rock and hide. But instead of letting failure get us down, we can choose to laugh at ourselves, learn from our mistakes, and keep moving forward. Because at the end of the day, it's not about how many times we fall, but how many times we get back up, dust ourselves off, and keep going.

So, if life gives you lemons, make lemonade. And if you spill that lemonade, laugh, clean up the mess, and make some more. Because that's what it's all about - finding the humor in our mishaps, learning from our failures, and never giving up on our pursuit of success, no matter how many ladders we have to climb.

In the following chapters, we'll explore more funny stories of unexpected failures, and share strategies for laughing at yourself, learning from your mistakes, and keeping a positive attitude in the face of adversity. Because when you can learn to laugh at yourself and find the humor in life's mishaps, there's no failure too great that you can't overcome.

Chapter 2
The Ladder of Success is Actually a Jungle Gym

In the grand tradition of career advice, someone (probably a guy named Chad) once told me, "If you want to get ahead, you have to climb the corporate ladder. It's simple math: start at the bottom, put in the work, and eventually, you'll reach the top rung." Sounds easy, right? Except, I kept getting poked in the eye by splinters, and those "rungs" felt suspiciously like pointy lies.

The thing is, we've all been fed this image of success as a sleek, silver ladder. It's clean, predictable, and only has one way up. But let me tell you, my actual career path has looked more like a kindergartener's jungle gym – a little wobbly, often upside-down, and occasionally featuring a stray goldfish cracker.

I'm not alone in this. Think about the most interesting people you know (not you, obviously, you're already interesting, or you wouldn't be reading this). How many of them took a straight, ladder-like path to get where they are? My guess is, not many. Success has a million different blueprints, and most of them involve a few detours through the ball pit of failure.

So, what does this jungle gym of success look like? Well, for me, it meant starting in journalism, swinging over to marketing, doing a few loop-the-loops in non-profit work, and finally, monkey-bar-ing my way into writing books that (fingers crossed) make people laugh and think a little.

Your jungle gym will be different. Maybe it's got a fireman's pole of promotions, or a see-saw of side-hustles, or even a sandbox where you're building something entirely new. The point is, there's no one "right" way up. And honestly, who wants to reach the top of a ladder anyway? It's all precarious and windy up there.

Embrace the wobble of your jungle gym. The best views in life are often from the part of the playground no one told you to climb. So, go ahead, grab the next rung (or is it a handle? or a rope? you get the idea...), and keep swinging. Your unique brand of success is waiting, and it's probably going to be way more fun than some boring old ladder.

Chapter 3: I Meant to Step on the First Rung, But I Missed

I'm not sure what's more astonishing – the number of times I've tripped over my own feet on the way to success, or how often I've blamed the ladder. Picture this: I'm standing in front of the gleaming Ladder of Ambition, ready to ascend to greatness. I stretch out my hand confidently, aiming for that first rung... and miss it by a mile. My fingers close on air as I stumble forward, nearly face-planting into the ladder.

It's not the ladder's fault. It's right there, sturdy and inviting. The problem is me – and my ongoing battle with procrastination. I'm the master of finding creative ways to avoid actually starting. I can turn a simple task into an Olympic sport of delay and distraction. I've wasted entire days "preparing" to work – reorganizing my desk drawers, trying out different pens, reading "inspirational" quotes until I feel too guilty to put off my task any longer.

Take writing this book, for example. I knew I had a great idea, and the passion to make it happen. But did I sit down and start typing out my brilliant prose?

Nope. First, I spent an hour crafting the perfect writing playlist. I mean, you can't create something amazing while listening to subpar music, right? Then I realized my desk could really use organizing. It's hard to focus amidst clutter. And I was definitely too thirsty to think clearly – better get that glass of water. Oh, and I should probably check email... you never know when something urgent will come up. Before I knew it, hours had vanished, and the only words in my document were "Chapter 1:" followed by a lot of stares at a blinking cursor.

Procrastination is like that – sneaky, persuasive, and determined to keep you at the bottom of the ladder. It's a master of disguise, dressing up excuses in convincing logic. "I work better under pressure," it tells me, as I put off a task until the last minute. "I need a break," it whispers, as I click away from my work to scroll mindlessly through social media.

But I've learned a few tricks for outsmarting it. Well, "learned" might be too strong a word. Let's say I'm still in the process of learning, with occasional successes and frequent face-plants back into old habits. The key is to understand that procrastination isn't the enemy – it's just a (really annoying) part of the process. Everyone deals with it, even the people who seem to effortlessly climb the Ladder of Success. The difference is, they've learned to laugh at their own antics, trick themselves into taking that first step, and keep moving upward, one rung at a time.

Here's one strategy that sometimes works: I trick myself into starting. I tell myself, "Just work on this for 10 minutes. That's it. If you still hate it after 10 minutes, you can quit." Of course, once I've started, I usually get engrossed and want to keep going. It's like that old advice to get yourself to the gym – once you're there, you might as well work out. But that first step (or in my case, the decision to open the document and type a single sentence) is the hardest.

Another trick is turning procrastination into a game. I challenge myself: How much can I get done before that cup of coffee is empty? Can I finish this section before my favorite song ends? It's absurd, but it works. Suddenly, the task stops feeling like a chore and becomes a fun little competition with myself. I've even been known to set a timer and try to write as much as possible in 25 minutes, just to see what I can accomplish.

    The most important thing I've learned is to be kind to myself. When I inevitably fall into old patterns and waste an hour on meaningless tasks, I try not to beat myself up over it. Instead, I acknowledge the procrastination, have a good laugh at my own expense, and gently nudge myself back on track. After all, the only way to reach the top of that ladder is to keep climbing – even if it's one awkward, stumbling step at a time.

    So if you're like me and you keep tripping over your own feet, don't worry. That ladder isn't going anywhere. Take a deep breath, dust yourself off, and try again. And remember, the only way to reach the top is to get started – even if that means starting with a really bad first sentence. With persistence, patience, and a sense of humor, you'll be climbing that ladder in no time.

Chapter 4: Who Needs a Ladder When You Have a Trampoline?

When I was a kid, I was always getting into trouble. Not the malicious kind, mind you, but the "curious and a little too adventurous" variety. Like the time I decided I could fly off the roof with a makeshift cape made from a trash bag and some twine. Or the afternoon I tried to "improve" my bicycle by removing a few parts I thought were unnecessary (spoiler alert: they were not unnecessary). Or who could forget the great "kitchen chemistry" experiment that ended with a mini explosion and a lot of smoke?

Looking back, those were some spectacular failures. The kind that leave you scraped up, crying, and vowing to never again attempt to defy gravity or play engineer without a license. But in the grand tapestry of my life, those failures became the threads of valuable lessons. I learned about perseverance (get back on that bike, even if it's harder to ride), creative problem-solving (maybe use more than twine next time), and the importance of a good helmet. I learned that failure, while it might sting in the moment, is not the end of the world. In fact, it's often just the beginning of something new.

Failure is Not the Opposite of Success, It's a Part Of It

Our culture loves a good success story. We put people on pedestals when they achieve something amazing and then... we often forget to tell the rest of the story. The part where they stumbled, fell, and sometimes face-planted along the way. We gloss over the failures, the setbacks, the moments of doubt and fear, as if those parts weren't equally important. We make it seem like success is a straight, easy climb up a ladder, rung by rung, no sweat broken.

But failure is not some shameful step-sibling of success. It's a teammate. A co-conspirator. Sometimes, it's even the coach, yelling at us to get back out there and try harder. Every successful person has a catalog of failures in their rearview mirror. J.K. Rowling, creator of the billion-dollar Harry Potter franchise, was a single mom living on welfare when she began writing. Walt Disney was fired from a newspaper job for "lacking creativity." Henry Ford's early businesses failed and left him broke five times before he built the Ford Motor Company. Thomas Edison is famous for saying, "I have not failed. I've just found 10,000 ways that won't work." when asked about his many attempts at inventing the light bulb.

Embracing Failure as a Trampoline

So, how do we start to embrace failure in a way that propels us forward instead of holding us back? Here are a few ideas:

Reframe Failure as an Opportunity: Instead of beating yourself up over a mistake, ask what you can learn from it. What would you do differently next time? Where is the chance to grow?

Celebrate the Attempt: It takes guts to try something new, even if it doesn't work out. Acknowledge that courage, whether it's in yourself or someone else. Have a "failing forward" party and share stories of times you gave it a go, even if you didn't quite hit the mark.
Don't Be Afraid to Look Silly: Some of the best learning experiences start with taking a risk and ending up in a heap. Think of it as

research. Embrace the absurdity and laugh at yourself.
Get Back to Work: Don't give up. Keep experimenting, keep pushing.

    Remember, failure is not a permanent address, just a temporary stop on the journey. Failure is not the end of the road. It's a detour, a rest stop, maybe even a shortcut in disguise. It's a chance to catch your breath, readjust, and launch again with new knowledge and a bit more wisdom. It's a trampoline that can propel us higher than we ever could have climbed on our own.

So, who needs a ladder when you have a trampoline? A ladder might help you climb slowly and carefully to the top, but a trampoline... that's how you can bounce back, soar higher, and maybe even fly (just don't forget the helmet).

Chapter 5: I Think I Climbed the Wrong Ladder...

As I sat atop what I thought was the pinnacle of success, sipping my lukewarm coffee in a corner office with a view that only pigeons would envy, it dawned on me—I think I climbed the wrong ladder.

You see, there's this unwritten rule in life: never trust a ladder handed to you by someone else, especially if it's made of flimsy promises and societal expectations. But there I was, halfway up this ladder of success, realizing it was leaning against the wrong wall.

It's a peculiar feeling, realizing you're on the wrong path. It's like ordering a burger only to realize you're actually a vegetarian. You question every decision you've made, every step you've taken, and wonder if there's a cosmic reset button you can press.

So, I did what any rational person would do in that situation—I panicked. I mean, who wouldn't? It's like waking up in the middle of the ocean on a deflating rubber duck floaty, realizing you forgot your sunscreen and snacks.

But then, amidst the chaos of my existential crisis, a glimmer of hope emerged—a tiny lifeboat in the form of introspection. I realized that being lost is just an opportunity to find a new path, preferably one with less questionable ladders and more solid ground.

First, I had to accept the fact that I had veered off course. Denial is like trying to navigate a maze blindfolded—it only leads to more dead ends and frustration. So, I embraced my confusion like a long-lost friend who shows up uninvited but brings good snacks.

Next, I took inventory of my goals, dreams, and aspirations. It's like cleaning out your closet—you have to sift through the clutter to find the gems buried beneath the outdated fashion trends and mismatched socks. I asked myself the tough questions: What do I really want? What makes me happy? And most importantly, why am I still wearing socks with holes in them?

Then came the hard part—charting a new course. It's like trying to navigate a GPS without a signal—you have to rely on your instincts and hope you don't end up in a ditch. I explored different options, considered new paths, and even entertained the idea of becoming a professional dog walker (hey, stranger things have happened).

But ultimately, I found my way. It wasn't easy, and there were plenty of detours and U-turns along the road, but I eventually stumbled upon a path that felt right—a path that wasn't dictated by society's expectations or someone else's definition of success.

I started small, dipping my toes into different ventures and hobbies. I took pottery classes, tried my hand at gardening, and even dabbled in stand-up comedy (though the less said about that, the better). Each experience taught me something new about myself and helped me inch closer to finding my true calling.

And then, one day, it happened. I stumbled upon a passion project that lit a fire in my soul—a project that combined my love for storytelling with my knack for problem-solving. It was like finding the missing puzzle piece that completed the picture of my life.

So, if you ever find yourself halfway up a ladder only to realize it's the wrong one, don't despair. Embrace the confusion, reassess your goals, and forge a new path— one that's uniquely yours. And who knows, maybe you'll end up discovering a hidden talent for dog whispering along the way. After all, life is too short to climb someone else's ladder. It's time to build your own.

Chapter 6: Success is Like Finding a Ladder in a Haystack

As you stumble through the dense thicket of setbacks and disappointments, it's easy to feel like success is a distant dream, buried beneath a mountain of failures. But what if I told you that success isn't some elusive treasure hidden deep within the caverns of adversity? What if, instead, it's more like finding a ladder in a haystack?

Let me paint you a picture. Imagine you're in a vast field of golden hay, surrounded by endless possibilities but also countless obstacles. You're desperately searching for that ladder to climb out of the pit of failure when suddenly, against all odds, you stumble upon it.

But here's the catch: the ladder wasn't placed there by

some benevolent force or stroke of luck. No, it was there all along, camouflaged by the straw and the challenges you faced. Success, much like that ladder, is often hiding in plain sight, waiting for you to shift your perspective and see the opportunities amidst the chaos.

    I remember a time when I felt utterly defeated, like I was

drowning in a sea of setbacks. I had poured my heart and soul into a project, only to watch it crumble before my eyes. But in the midst of my despair, I stumbled upon a comedic twist of fate that changed everything.

You see, as I was wallowing in self-pity, I received a call from a friend inviting me to a comedy show. Despite my initial reluctance, I decided to go, if only to distract myself from my troubles. Little did I know, that night would become a turning point in my journey towards success.

As I laughed until tears streamed down my cheeks, I realized something profound: amidst the rubble of my failures, there was still so much joy to be found. That comedy show wasn't just a temporary escape; it was a reminder that even in the darkest of times, there are moments of lightness and laughter waiting to be discovered.

It was in that moment of clarity that I realized success isn't just about achieving your goals; it's about finding joy and gratitude in the journey, no matter how rocky the road may be. Like finding a needle in a haystack, success often requires patience, perseverance, and a keen eye for the silver linings hidden within the clouds.

As I sat in the audience, surrounded by the contagious energy of laughter, I couldn't help but marvel at the irony of the situation. Here I was, nursing a bruised ego and battered spirit, finding solace in the unlikeliest of places—a comedy show. It was as if the universe had orchestrated this moment specifically for me, a gentle nudge to remind me that life, despite its many twists and turns, is still worth celebrating.

As the comedian on stage riffed on the absurdities of everyday life, I found myself nodding along in agreement, my troubles momentarily forgotten in the sea of shared laughter. It was cathartic, almost surreal, to realize that amidst the chaos of my failures, there existed moments of pure joy and camaraderie.

But it wasn't just the comedy that lifted my spirits that night; it was the people surrounding me, strangers brought together by a shared appreciation for humor and humanity. In their laughter and applause, I found a sense of belonging, a reminder that I wasn't alone in my struggles.

As the show came to an end and we spilled out onto the bustling city streets, I felt lighter, rejuvenated even. It was as if a weight had been lifted off my shoulders, replaced by a newfound sense of hope and optimism.

In the days that followed, I found myself reflecting on that transformative evening, drawing strength from its unexpected lessons. I realized that success isn't just about achieving lofty goals or reaching the pinnacle of your career—it's about finding joy and meaning in the everyday moments, no matter how small or insignificant they may seem.

Armed with this newfound perspective, I approached my challenges with renewed vigor and determination. Instead of dwelling on my failures, I focused on the lessons they taught me and the opportunities they presented. And slowly but surely, I began to see progress, inching closer to my goals with each passing day.

    Looking back on that night, I can't help but marvel at the serendipity of it all. Who would have thought that a comedy show would hold the key to unlocking my potential and reshaping my outlook on success? But therein lies the beauty of life—it's full of surprises, both big and small, waiting to be discovered by those willing to embrace them with open arms.

So, dear reader, the next time you find yourself lost in the midst of failure and uncertainty, remember this: success is not a destination to be reached, but a journey to be embraced. And sometimes, all it takes is a shift in perspective to uncover the ladder of success hidden in the haystack of life.

Chapter 7: I Finally Reached the Top of the Ladder and It Was a Letdown

As I climbed the rungs of the proverbial ladder of success, I often fantasized about how amazing it would feel to finally reach the top. I envisioned fireworks, confetti, maybe even a marching band playing my favorite tune. But let me tell you, dear reader, the reality was far from glamorous.

After years of relentless hustle, sleepless nights, and enough coffee to fill a swimming pool, I finally found myself perched at the summit of success. And you know what I saw? Absolutely nothing. Well, nothing except for a vast expanse of empty space and a nagging sense of emptiness in my gut.

I had achieved all the goals I set out to accomplish. I had the corner office, the fat paycheck, and the fancy title to match. But instead of feeling elated, I felt like I was starring in my own personal episode of "Is That All There Is?"

I couldn't help but wonder if I had been chasing the wrong dreams all along. Had I been so focused on climbing the ladder that I forgot to check if it was even leaning against the right wall?

As I sat there, contemplating my existence atop the ladder of success, I realized something profound: achievement alone doesn't guarantee fulfillment. Sure, reaching your goals is important, but it's what you do with those achievements that truly matters.

So, I decided to take a step back and reassess my priorities. I started asking myself some tough questions: What truly makes me happy? What am I passionate about? What kind of legacy do I want to leave behind?

And you know what I discovered? It wasn't the corner

office or the fat paycheck that brought me joy; it was the little moments of connection, the simple pleasures of life, and the pursuit of something greater than myself.

With this newfound clarity, I set out on a journey to find meaning and purpose beyond just achieving goals. I started volunteering at a local charity, spending more time with loved ones, and pursuing hobbies that brought me genuine joy.

And you know what? It was liberating. I may have left the ladder of success behind, but I found something far more valuable: fulfillment.

So, to anyone out there who's feeling disillusioned atop their own ladder of success, I offer you this advice: take a step back, reassess your priorities, and remember that true fulfillment comes from living a life aligned with your values and passions, not just ticking off boxes on a checklist.

And who knows? You might just find that the view from the top of a different ladder is even better than you ever imagined.

The realization hit me like a ton of bricks: I had spent so much time chasing after success that I never stopped to consider if it was what I truly wanted. It was like ordering a gourmet meal, only to find out it was missing the secret ingredient that made it truly satisfying.

So, there I was, perched atop the ladder of success, staring into the abyss of my own dissatisfaction. It was the ultimate "Is That All There Is?" moment, complete with a soundtrack of existential dread playing on repeat in my mind.

But amidst the disappointment, a tiny spark of realization flickered to life. Maybe, just maybe, the problem wasn't with the ladder itself, but rather with my expectations of what awaited me at the top. I had bought into the myth that success was the ultimate destination, the golden ticket to everlasting happiness and fulfillment. But as I stood there, surveying the landscape of my achievements, I couldn't shake the feeling that something was missing.

It dawned on me that perhaps true fulfillment wasn't about reaching a specific destination, but rather about the journey itself. It wasn't about the shiny trophies lining my office shelves or the digits in my bank account; it was about the moments, the connections, the experiences that made life worth living.

With this epiphany came a flood of questions. What was I truly passionate about? What brought me joy beyond the confines of my job title? What legacy did I want to leave behind, not just in terms of career success, but in terms of the impact I had on others and the world around me?

As I grappled with these questions, I realized that I had been neglecting the things that truly mattered to me in pursuit of societal markers of success. I had sacrificed time with loved ones, neglected my own well-being, and put my passions on the back burner, all in the name of climbing the ladder.

But now, standing at the summit, I saw clearly that the ladder of success was just one piece of the puzzle. True fulfillment lay in living a life aligned with my values, pursuing my passions wholeheartedly, and making meaningful connections along the way.

So, I made a choice. I made the decision to step off the ladder of conventional success and forge my own path. I started by redefining my priorities, carving out time for the things that brought me joy, and nurturing relationships that filled my soul.

I volunteered at church, rediscovered my love for writing, and spent lazy Sundays with family and friends, relishing in the simple pleasures of life. And with each step away from the ladder, I felt a weight lift off my shoulders, replaced by a sense of freedom and authenticity.

Sure, the view from the top of the ladder of success may have been a letdown, but the view from where I stood now – surrounded by love, passion, and purpose – was nothing short of breathtaking. And as I gazed out at the horizon, I knew that I had finally found what I had been searching for all along: true fulfillment, not at the top of a ladder, but in the journey of self-discovery and living a life true to myself.

Chapter 8: Maybe the Ladder Was Just a Suggestion

As I stood amidst the wreckage of my failed attempts at climbing the traditional ladder of success, I couldn't help but feel a twinge of frustration. The path I had chosen, the milestones I had meticulously aimed for, all

seemed like futile efforts now.
Yet, in that moment of
disillusionment, a spark of
realization ignited within me –
perhaps the ladder wasn't the only
means to ascend.

Success, as I had once
perceived it, was a linear journey,
a relentless climb towards an
elusive summit dictated by
societal norms and expectations.

But as I surveyed the landscape of my own aspirations, I began to see it differently. It wasn't a rigid structure with predetermined rungs; it was more like a vast, untamed wilderness, teeming with opportunities and hidden trails waiting to be explored. Maybe, just maybe, the ladder was merely a suggestion – a well-intentioned guide, but not the definitive path to the top.

Determined to redefine success on my own terms, I embarked on a quest to unearth stories of unconventional triumphs – those moments when individuals dared to defy convention and carve their own paths to greatness. What I discovered were tales of resilience, creativity, and unwavering determination, often intertwined with humor and unexpected twists.

Take the story of Sarah, for instance, a struggling artist who found herself grappling with the closed doors of the traditional gallery scene. Undeterred by rejection, she decided to showcase her vibrant paintings in the most unlikely of venues – a cozy corner of her neighborhood coffee shop. Little did she know, her whimsical depictions of cats adorned in bowties would capture the imagination of coffee aficionados and art enthusiasts alike. Before she knew it, Sarah's once-overlooked corner became a bustling hub of creativity, her paintings flying off the walls faster than she could paint them. In the process, she not only redefined the concept of a gallery but also proved that success knows no boundaries.

    Then there's the tale of Mike, a self-professed tech geek who spent years navigating the treacherous waters of Silicon Valley in pursuit of corporate recognition. Frustrated by the relentless competition and stifling bureaucracy, he made a bold decision – to abandon the safety of the established order and embark on a journey of self-discovery. Armed with little more than a laptop and a fervent passion for all things digital, Mike launched his own tech blog, where he shared his insights and musings with the world. What started as a humble endeavor soon blossomed into a thriving online community, attracting like-minded individuals from every corner of the globe. Today, Mike's blog not only serves as a platform for innovation and discourse but also as a testament to the power of authenticity and perseverance.

These stories, and countless others like them, serve as a poignant reminder that success is not a destination; it's a journey — a deeply personal voyage fueled by passion, determination, and a willingness to defy convention. It's about embracing the uniqueness of your own narrative, celebrating the quirks and idiosyncrasies that make you who you are. So, to all the dreamers and strivers out there, I implore you to look beyond the confines of the traditional ladder and embrace the vast expanse of possibility that lies before you. Who knows? Maybe the ladder was just a suggestion all along – a gentle nudge in the right direction, but ultimately, it's up to you to chart your own course.

Chapter 9: Recap

Maybe the Ladder Was Just a Suggestion As we journey through life, we often encounter obstacles that seem insurmountable. The metaphorical ladder of success, once believed to be our ticket to the top, becomes a tangled mess of uncertainty and confusion. But fear not, dear reader, for in the midst of chaos lies opportunity, and perhaps the ladder was never the only path to greatness after all.

In our quest to conquer the world, we sometimes find ourselves taking unexpected detours, missing steps, or even stumbling upon entirely different routes. And you know what? That's perfectly okay. Life has a funny way of leading us where we need to go, even if it means veering off the beaten path.

In "When Life Gives You Lemons, Make Lemonade," we learned the importance of resilience and adaptability. Adversity may knock us down, but it's our ability to rise again, armed with humor and a positive outlook, that truly defines us.

"The Ladder of Success is Actually a Jungle Gym" reminded us that success is not a linear journey. It's a wild, unpredictable adventure filled with twists and turns, ups and downs. Embracing the chaos and learning to navigate the jungle gym of life with grace and humor is key to reaching our goals.

"I Meant to Step on the First Rung, But I Missed" taught us the value of perseverance and determination. Even when we veer off course or encounter setbacks, it's essential to keep moving forward, one step at a time, towards our dreams.

"Who Needs a Ladder When You Have a Trampoline?" challenged our preconceived notions of success. Sometimes, the traditional path isn't the right fit for us, and that's okay. Thinking outside the box, embracing our unique strengths, and taking unconventional leaps of faith can lead to unexpected triumphs.

"I Think I Climbed the Wrong Ladder..." reminded us to stay true to ourselves and our passions. Success means different things to different people, and it's essential to define our own version of success rather than conforming to societal expectations.

"Success is Like Finding a Ladder in a Haystack" encouraged us to embrace the journey, no matter how daunting it may seem. Life is full of challenges and uncertainties, but within every haystack, there's a hidden ladder waiting to be discovered.

"I Finally Reached the Top of the Ladder and It Was a Letdown" reminded us that true fulfillment comes from within. Achieving our goals is undoubtedly satisfying, but it's the journey, the growth, and the lessons learned along the way that truly enrich our lives.

And finally, "Maybe the Ladder Was Just a Suggestion" urged us to embrace uncertainty and trust in the process. Life is unpredictable, and there's beauty in the unknown. So, let go of rigid expectations, laugh in the face of adversity, and remember that sometimes, the best adventures begin when we step off the beaten path.

As we continue our journey, let's keep laughing, keep moving forward, and keep embracing the twists and turns that make life worth living. After all, who knows what extraordinary adventures lie ahead?

And in the wise words of the legendary comedian, Bob Hope: "I have seen what a laugh can do. It can transform almost unbearable tears into something bearable, even hopeful." So, let's keep laughing, my friends, for in laughter, we find strength, resilience, and endless possibilities.

So, here's to embracing life's chaos, finding joy in the journey, and making our own way in this wild and wonderful world. Cheers to the unexpected, the unconventional, and the downright hilarious moments that make life worth living. And remember, when in doubt, just keep climbing – or bouncing, or swinging – whatever works for you. After all, maybe the ladder was just a suggestion.

Sources:

- **Hope, Bob. "Bob Hope Quotes." BrainyQuote, Xplore, www.brainyquote.com/quotes/bob_hope_163137.**

Drew Wohlford always had dreams of becoming a scriptwriter but then life happened. His parents divorced shortly after high school, he attended St Francis College in Fort Wayne, Indiana after wandering aimlessly in life for years. Again he found his passion for writing being encouraged by Dr. L. Carl Nadeau, his creative writing teacher.

    Then life happened again, he met his wife, Brenda. Soon there were kids and then grandkids. There were numerous jobs of all kinds, as he tried to find his passion, but it had been put on a back burner. Then in November of 2020, Drew was hit with COVID-19, which turned into long COVID and without work, and facing his 60th birthday, Drew didn't look back, he looked forward and thought, it's now or never. With a laptop in hand, he began to document the stories he told his grandchildren. The passion had once again been ignited.

Discover These Other Great Books By Author Drew Wohlford on AMAZON

Discover These Other Great Books By Author Drew Wohlford on AMAZON

Discover These Other Great Books By Author Drew Wohlford on AMAZON

www.ingramcontent.com/pod-product-compliance
Lightning Source LLC
Chambersburg PA
CBHW050115230526
45470CB00004B/1836